DIESEL SPECTRUM

Volume 5

NEW SOUTH WALES

The Candy Era

Peter Attenborough

Photos by the author unless otherwise credited

Published April 2000 by

Eveleigh Press

ACN 000 558 574

PO Box 345

Matraville NSW 2036

Phone: (02) 9311 2036

National Library of Australia Card Number and

ISBN 1 876568 08 9

Production by Peter Attenborough, John Casey and Bob Gallagher with assistance from Karen Baldini.

Typeset by the publishers and
printed in Hong Kong by
Phoenix Offset

Standing beneath looming sandstone cliffs at the eastern end of Marrangaroo tunnel with No.M312 works train on 6 June 1986, 4918 displays the typical way in which the horizontal stripes of the Candy livery were applied to the running board and the lower section of the hood side. On all hood units, except the 73 class, the 'double-seven' logos were placed on the cab side, below the windows.

Introduction

At a gathering at Sydney Terminal station on 17 August 1982, the State Rail Authority of New South Wales (SRA) unveiled its new corporate livery for locomotives, railcars and country passenger rollingstock. Presented to the public and media that day were several passenger vehicles and diesel-electric locomotive 44100, all displaying the vibrant colours of red, with varying width horizontal stripes of white, orange and yellow. Designed by the late Phil Belbin, this striking pattern soon earned the nickname of the Candy livery. For almost ten years, these colours were progressively applied to many locomotives and much of the SRA's country passenger rollingstock.

As with any colour scheme, variations inevitably occurred. Differences in the colour used on the roof varied not only between classes but also between members of the same class of locomotive. The width of the coloured stripes, in particular the white stripe, and the colour and position of logos were other anomalies to appear on those Candy-liveried locomotives.

Many of these variations are depicted on the following pages. During the ten years that the Candy pattern was in vogue, a number of locomotives were painted in those colours for a second time. In some cases, this repainting resulted in minor differences emerging, such as a change in the colour of logos. The only class of diesel-electric locomotives to enter service painted in the Candy colours were the initial batch of Clyde-built 81s (8101-8180). Virtually all other classes of mainline, branchline and shunting diesel-electric and diesel-hydraulic locomotives, then in service, had at least one representative painted in the Candy livery.

Following the introduction of the Freight Rail blue colour scheme from the early 1990s, the Candy design began to disappear until, by the end of 1999, only 42203 remained in regular service wearing Phil Belbin's striking livery.

Acknowledgments

Thanks are extended to the following people who have assisted with the production of this volume of Diesel Spectrum, either by supplying photographs or providing editorial comment, particularly Graham Attenborough, Alex Foot, Bruce Freeman, Ray Love, Roger Renton and David Staunton.

Candy Painted Locomotives

42101, 42102, 42103, 42105, 42106, 42107, 42108
42202, 42203, 42204, 42205, 42206, 42208-42219
4403, 4405, 4406, 4419, 4424, 4428, 4431, 4432, 4438, 4439, 4451, 4460
4461, 4463-4468, 4471, 4472, 4474, 4477, 4483, 4492, 4495, 4496, 4499, 44100
4501-4504, 4506, 4510, 4512, 4514-4524, 4526-4528, 4530, 4531, 4533-4536, 4538, 4539
44201-44240 (excluding 44232)
4701-4708, 4712, 4714, 4717, 4718, 4720
4808, 4811, 4827, 4833, 4834, 4838, 4839, 4841-4850, 4852-4855, 4857, 4859, 4869, 4874, 4875, 4881, 4889, 4891, 48100, 48103, 48106-48108, 48110, 48115, 48117, 48119-48122, 48124-48164
4902, 4903, 4905, 4907-4910, 4912, 4913, 4914, 4916, 4918
8015, 8018, 8034
8101-8180
7007
7301-7303, 7310, 7312, 7314-7320, 7322, 7324, 7325, 7327, 7328, 7331, 7335, 7336
X101
X203, X204, X215

One of four 421s painted with a grey roof, 42107 is shown hauling a failed DEB railcar set forming No.SR37 Canberra-Monaro Express away from Gib tunnel near Bowral on 14 March 1986. This locomotive varied from other grey-roofed 421s by having a yellow 'double-seven' logo.

Variations from the normal specifications on 42107 include an exceptionally wide white stripe, road numbers painted beneath the No.2-end cab windows, side number applied near roof level and the position of the tail disc. Management were not impressed and 42107 was sent back to the paint shop.   David Staunton, Bruce Freeman collection

Like several other classes of locomotive, the colour applied to the roof of the 421s varied between class members. On 14 December 1986, grey-roofed 42103 approaches Picton with No.SL20 passenger. This particular 421 has white 'double-seven' logos.
Graham Attenborough

This view shows the opposite side of 42103 to that above. Of interest is the different position of the locomotive numbers on the side of the carbody. Taken on 26 April 1986, freshly painted 42103 leads 42109 on No.3462 goods near Enfield South, its grey roof yet to become discoloured by exhaust emissions.

Three 421s received a red roof when painted in the Candy livery. Recently overhauled, and displaying that colour roof, 42101 departs Thirroul with No.CL36 passenger on 13 December 1983. Of interest is the extraordinarily wide white stripe and the location of the white-painted number on the observer's side of the No.2-end of this locomotive.

In pristine external condition after overhaul, red-roofed 42102 leads Indian red-liveried 42103 out of Gib tunnel near Bowral on 11 January 1985, with No.1415 goods. The white stripe on 42102 is of normal width, while the pilot is unusual in that it has been painted white.

All 422s received a grey roof when painted into the Candy livery. On 1 May 1993, 42213/4454/4823 pass Bundanoon with No.2339 goods. When first painted in Candy colours, 42213 had yellow 'double-seven' logos, but when painted for a second time, white logos were applied.

The only member of its class so painted, 42202 displays mini-numbers on the end of its cabs. It is shown leading 42208/42220 on No.GK33 coal train at Maldon on 22 April 1990. The colour of the 'double-seven' logos varies between each of the Candy-liveried 422s on this train.

Not long after being painted Candy, 42208 ascends Spaniards Hill near Menangle with No.3462 express goods on 1 October 1983. This was the standard Candy pattern applied to 422 class locomotives at the time, the colour of the logos being changed from yellow to white on several class members some years later.

Candy-liveried 422s also saw interstate service. During the 1980s, 422s regularly worked into Victoria. On 11 January 1986, 42219 leads V/Line T411 into Albury yard with a goods from Melbourne. Of interest is the grey roof of the 422, which has become heavily discoloured.

On 17 February 1989, 42211 stands on the down main line at Picton with No.3472 goods to allow another service to overtake. White has been used extensively around the windows, while the window frames are black to reduce reflected glare.

By the end of 1999, 42203 was the sole remaining Candy locomotive in regular service. Dedicated to Countrylink passenger services, it shared these duties with Indian red-liveried 42220. On 24 July 1999, 42203 descends the Cullarin range with No.SL15 Griffith passenger. The blue panel forward of the rear cab covers the air-conditioning unit that was fitted earlier in 1999.

A number of first-series 44 class were painted in the Candy pattern, including 4451 shown passing through Mittagong in company with reverse-liveried 4471 on 27 March 1986. The train is No.2W47 empty mill wheat which, on this day, was also conveying several goods vehicles.

Standing in the up refuge siding at Wingello on 11 April 1986, No.2660 limestone train, being hauled by 4438/44201, is overtaken by No.ST22 XPT. Of interest are the black numbers painted above each of the cab windows at the No.2-end of the 44 class.

Having not long emerged from the paint shop, an immaculate 4428 leads 4463 on No.1101 empty coal train to Wallerawang Colliery on 22 August 1986. The cleanliness of the grey roof and 'double-seven' logos on 4428 contrasts with those on 4463.

Hauling a consist of Tuscan-liveried cars, 4403 works up Cowan bank with No.N66 passenger on 24 September 1983. Despite having been painted in the Candy colours for only several months, 4403 has already become very dirty.

This view of 4496 on No.2555 cement train, taken at Maldon on 9 May 1986, depicts what could be termed the normal pattern used on Candy 44 class locomotives. The use of white edging around the windows, both at the No.1- and No.2-end, the white 'double-seven' logos and the width of the Candy stripes, is all typical.

Running No.2-end leading, 4463, in company with 4468, works No.2676 clinker train near Bargo, on 3 January 1991. White is used from just below the windows to the roof line, while the locomotive numbers are in illuminated number boxes above each window at the No.2-end on these later series 44 class locomotives.

Three identically painted Candy 44s, 4483/44100/4467, pass through Monkerai with No.6319 goods on 15 April 1988. The stripes on all locomotives are perfectly aligned, although the cleanliness of this particular trio does not portray a good image for their owners.

Several Candy 44 class locomotives had yellow 'double-seven' logos. This was normal practice during the first few years of the Candy era. As time went by, white was adopted as standard. On 31 August 1988, and with each locomotive displaying a different coloured logo, 4466/44100 approach Allandale with No.5329 empty wheat train.

The sole member of the Candy-liveried 45 class to have a white roof was 4504. On 9 September 1983, it leads Indian red 4535 on a loaded coal train at Tighes Hill. The stripes on Candy 45 and 48 class locomotives were broken where they crossed the side of the cab.

On 5 March 1984, 4514/4406 depart Port Waratah with No.1619 empty wheat train. This 45 class locomotive was typical of the majority of its Candy brethren in that it had a red roof. It was considered that red did not show the dirt as quickly as other colours that were used.

Several 45 class had grey roofs. A very weathered 4517 departs Port Botany with a load of containers on 21 June 1986. Its grey roof is covered in grime from the exhaust while the side of the hood shows evidence of oil leakages.

There were two variations of grey roof used on the Candy 45 class. Sea grey was applied only to one member of the class, 4516. It is shown on an up goods train near East Maitland on 4 February 1984. Grey covers not only the entire roof but also extends down on to the top of the hood sides. *Alex Foot*

On 7 October 1988, No.SL20 passenger approaches Aylmerton behind 44240. Although the manner in which the Candy livery was applied to members of the 442 class was relatively consistent, some variations occurred with numbers and logos. Here, 44240 has a yellow 'double-seven' logo.

Towards the end of their service life, the external condition of many 442 class locomotives deteriorated. A very shabby 44222, with numbers barely discernible, commences its descent of the Illawarra escarpment near Ocean View with No.PW02 wheat train on 29 July 1994. It is assisted by 4515 and 44237.

Apart from a discoloured roof, 44211 is in a fairly clean state as it eases to a halt at Kilbride loop with No.6184 goods on 22 November 1989. Like most Candy 442s, 44211 has white logos.

Several 442 class had mini-numbers applied on the front of their cabs. One of those was 44213, seen here assisting 4463 on No.6395 steel train near Hilldale on 14 August 1992. Although the window surrounds are painted white, black is used on the window frames.

Displaying larger than normal locomotive numbers on the end of the short hood, 4706 leads 4868/4882/48100 on No.P429 empty Pelton coal train through Weston on 4 July 1989. This locomotive was the only one of its class to have numbers of that size.

Surrounded by other Candy-liveried locomotives, 4708 stands at Broadmeadow depot on 9 June 1985. The white stripe was usually placed on the edge of the running board of hood units while the orange and yellow stripes were applied to the hood panels.
Graham Attenborough

The application of the colours on the Candy 47 class locomotives was uniform across almost the entire class. The use of white around the windows was more noticeable on the 47 class due to their large cab profile. On 18 August 1986, No.P421 empty coal train arrives at Pelton behind 4705/4702/4704.

Despite being heavily discoloured by exhaust fumes, 48121 displays its silver/grey roof. Only four 48s received this colour roof (48103, 48107, 48121 and 48125). The locomotive is departing Thirroul with a northbound local train on 10 September 1984. At this time, several sets of double-deck electric suburban trailer cars were augmenting traditional locomotive-hauled stock.

Another of the silver/grey roofed 48s, 48103, passes through Rhodes on 5 November 1983, with a mixed collection of rollingstock destined for the carriage sheds at Hornsby. A blue and white single-deck electric suburban car forms part of the consist.

The only 48 class locomotive to receive a white roof was 4833. It is shown approaching Neath on 29 September 1989, with 4898/48116/4890 on a loaded coal train from Pelton. The use of lighter colours on the roof was counterproductive due to the effects of exhaust emissions.
Alex Foot

Standing in the loop at Mindaribba on 4 December 1987, 48117 heads No.6121 stock special. This 48 class was the only member of its class to have a grey roof. The small platform at this isolated location has since been moved adjacent to the crossing loop.

This view of the No.2-end of 4842 shows the manner in which the Candy stripes wrap around the end of the long hood. The locomotive numbers are placed high, just below the headlights and handrail. The train is No.SL52 and it is nearing Berrima Junction on 14 March 1986.

Several Candy-liveried 48s line up at Delec on 26 July 1987. The uniformity in the way the Candy colours were applied is evident in this view. The locomotives are 48151, 48154, 48121, 48156 and 48143.   *Graham Attenborough*

No.3W98 mill wheat train climbs towards Exeter on 22 June 1990, behind 4842/4851/4829. The lead 48 is painted in Candy colours, while 4851 is adorned in the austere red-terror livery which followed the Candy design. The trailing locomotive is painted in the reverse pattern which preceded the Candy livery.

With any standard design, the occasional variation occurs. Here 4849 passes through Mittagong on 8 July 1992, with No.2448 cement train. Note the 'double-seven' logos beneath the drivers' cab window have been applied back-to-front. The locomotive is fitted with an exhaust scrubber.
Graham Attenborough

The Candy members of the 49 class presented several variations to the basic design. Here 4907 leads 4912 into Port Botany with No.T222 trip train on 28 April 1990. Compare the all-white valance of 4907 to the white and black pattern on 4912. Furthermore, 4907 has a smaller than usual white 'double-seven' logo on the cab side.

The most 'non-standard' Candy 49 class locomotive was 4910, seen here with 4901 at Darling Island on No.T34 trip train on 13 August 1990. Painted in a deeper red, 4910 had an all-white valance, no numbers on the end of the short hood, white logos, a red roof and red and silver pilot. It also lacked white around the windows.

Representative of most Candy-liveried 49 class were 4903/4902. They are shown working No.7004 goods near Pipers Flat on 17 October 1986. Both have a grey roof, yellow logos on the side of the cab and black and white stripes along the valance.

On 30 June 1990, 4908 shunts wagons for the Kellogg's factory at the Gelco sidings, near Botany, with No.T87 trip train. Adorned in the standard Candy livery, 4908 has white around the cab windows but with black on the window frames.

Having worn numerous colour schemes during its life, X101 stands outside the railway training college at Petersham on 15 September 1985, painted in the Candy design. White was used extensively, including the pilots, extended cab and handrails.
Graham Attenborough

Only one 70 class diesel-hydraulic locomotive was painted in the Candy colours, that being 7007. It is shown stored at Port Kembla depot on 31 October 1986, together with Indian red-liveried 7003, 7001, 7005 and 7004. Small numbers have been applied to the cab side.
Graham Attenborough

The X200 class rail tractors were well known for being painted in a wide range of liveries. However, only a few received the Candy colours. On 22 September 1989, Candy X204 shunts the once large yard at Coffs Harbour.

This view of X204 at Coffs Harbour, taken on 18 September 1989, depicts the silver and black pilot, lack of white locomotive numbers and logos, together with the use of yellow on the buffers. Only three X200s were painted in the Candy pattern.

The Candy 73 class differed from other Candy-painted hood units in that they did not have 'double-seven' logos applied on the cab sides. Instead, the locomotive number was placed in that position. On 23 March 1985, 7312/7310 approach Epping with a local trip working from Hornsby.   Alex Foot

Standing within the confines of Broadmeadow depot on 28 April 1984, 7328 and 4863 await their next roster. Note the white sandboxes on the running board, a feature of the Candy 73 class locomotives. The buffers on 7328 have been painted yellow to improve visibility.   Graham Attenborough

Two of the three Candy 80 class locomotives, 8015/8018, stand on the Austen and Butta siding at Wallerawang on 24 October 1992, with No.AK08 loaded coal train. All three Candy 80 class had grey roofs.

A down goods passes through the Southern highlands between Bundanoon and Penrose behind 8034/8030 on 5 October 1991. White 'double-seven' logos were used on the three Candy 80 class, as was a small Freight Rail logo beneath the observer's side window.
Graham Attenborough

Like the 422 class, 81 class locomotives worked into Victoria while painted in the Candy livery. Having exchanged with a 422 class which had brought the train from Melbourne, 8157 prepares to depart Albury with No.SL66 Intercapital Daylight Express on 2 March 1985.

The first ten 81 class were allocated to Broadmeadow depot for coal haulage in the Hunter Valley. In immaculate external condition, near-new 8110/8107 work No.MT313 empty coal train through Belford on 19 April 1983, bound for Mount Thorley.

The last of the original order of 81 class, 8180, approaches Wingello with No.3488 goods on 24 April 1986. The first eighty 81s were painted identically in the Candy livery when built by Clyde Engineering. The pilots on the 81 class locomotives were painted grey, whereas most other classes had their pilots painted silver or black.

When modifications were made to the exhaust systems of several 81 class locomotives, often a large white panel remained on the carbody side until painted some time later. On 1 December 1988, 8168/G523 near Tahmoor with No.3151 express goods. The white panel on 8168 is readily discernible.

Constant use in coal traffic resulted in most 81 class becoming dirty very quickly. Here 8122/8105 haul No.1739 loaded coal train through Thirroul on 27 November 1984. Due to modifications, there is a difference in the grille and porthole locations between each of these locomotives.